# TRAIL GRAZING

*40 High Energy Snacks to Fuel Your Adventures*

# TRAIL grazing

## 40 HIGH ENERGY SNACKS to FUEL your ADVENTURES

*Heather Legler*

Copyright ©2017 Heather Legler

*Dedicated to my husband and co-host, Josh. You are my favorite person.*

*Many thanks to the listeners of The First 40 Miles podcast. I continue to be amazed at how generous, kind, and supportive you are.*

*And special thanks to our team of 50 recipe testers. You made sure that the recipes in this book are trail-worthy!*

*Amanda Cook Hatfield*
*Amanda Zeller*
*Amy Cornish*
*Ashton Williams*
*David Williams*
*Dawn Rohm*
*Deanne Dwight*
*Diane Rhoads*
*Elizabeth Hall*
*Jack Eagling*
*Jessica Tufariello*
*Katie Raney*
*Kim Larson*
*Lauren Hughes*
*Levi Hodson*
*Mark Klauza*
*Mike Crafton*
*Nik Arini*
*Rebecca Wilson*
*Rob Ferguson*
*Robin Bass*
*Sarah Ulrich*
*Stefanie Pech*
*Stephanie Veteto*
*Vicki Knoer*

*And a few who wished to remain anonymous*

# Contents

Introduction .................................................................................................... 9
    Calories .................................................................................................... 10
    Getting Started ........................................................................................ 11
    What You'll Need .................................................................................... 11
    Keeping and Storing Your Snacks ......................................................... 13
    How Long Will My Snacks Last? ............................................................ 14
    Final Words ............................................................................................. 15

Bars + Bites ................................................................................................. 17
    Go-To Granola Bars ................................................................................ 18
    Perfect Crunchy Granola Bars ............................................................... 19
    Fruit + Nut Bars ....................................................................................... 20
    Quick Chocolate Caramel Bars .............................................................. 21
    Naturally Sweet + Chewy Baked Bars ................................................... 22
    Mini Chia Bars ......................................................................................... 23
    "Thoughtful" Bars .................................................................................... 24
    Big Batch Lunch Lady Bars .................................................................... 25
    Black Bean Brownies .............................................................................. 26
    Brownie Bark ........................................................................................... 27
    Whole Food Truffles ................................................................................ 28
    Hikers' Taffy ............................................................................................ 29

Fruit Leather ............................................................................................... 31
    Simple Fruit Leather ............................................................................... 32
    Berry + Beet Fruit Leather ...................................................................... 34
    Vanilla Orange Fruit Leather .................................................................. 35
    Cucumber + Lime Fruit Leather ............................................................. 36
    Yogurt Fruit Leather ................................................................................ 37

- Nuts + Seeds .................................................................................................... 39
  - Roasted Squash Seeds ................................................................................. 40
  - Coconut + Curry Cashews .......................................................................... 41
  - Smoky Maple BBQ Nuts ............................................................................. 42
  - Sesame Ginger Pecans ................................................................................ 43
  - Black Bean "Nuts" ....................................................................................... 44
  - Cocoa Dusted Almonds .............................................................................. 45
  - Montezuma's Chocolate Drops .................................................................. 46
- Whole Food Jerky ............................................................................................ 47
  - Beef + Veggie Jerky ..................................................................................... 48
  - California Jerky ........................................................................................... 50
  - Beef + Bean Burrito Jerky ........................................................................... 51
  - Thanksgiving Turkey Jerky ........................................................................ 52
  - Not Pemmican ............................................................................................. 53
  - Vegan + Gluten-free Pepperoni .................................................................. 54
- Breads + Crackers + Chips ............................................................................. 55
  - Plantain Chips ............................................................................................. 56
  - Flax Crackers ............................................................................................... 57
  - Veggie Crackers ........................................................................................... 58
  - Vollkornbrot Whole Rye Bread .................................................................. 59
  - Fruit and Nut Crostini ................................................................................ 60
- Microwave Muffins .......................................................................................... 61
  - Trail Cred Muffins ....................................................................................... 62
  - Blueberry Muffins ....................................................................................... 63
  - Cheesy Italian Muffins ................................................................................ 64
- Cheese ................................................................................................................ 65
  - Hand-Rubbed Artisan Cheese .................................................................... 66
  - "Everything Bagel" Mozzarella Cheese Sticks .......................................... 67
- About the Author ............................................................................................. 69
- Index .................................................................................................................. 70

# Introduction

Welcome to the wonderful world of trail grazing! Trail grazing is that delightful time on the trail between breakfast and dinner, where ne'er a fork or plate are seen, and the snacky goodness practically leaps out of your pack and unwraps itself in attempts to keep you fueled, fast, and happy while hiking.

Before I went on my first backpacking trip on the Timberline Trail in 2014, I understood lunch on the trail to be a casual picnic kind of affair in which we all lounged languidly and ate grapes like Romans. But I quickly realized that on the trail, there's too much to see and too many miles to cover to stop and whip out a blanket, a basket, and a bottle (let alone a toga) every time hunger strikes. Yes, trail grazing is a movable feast, and that feast has gotta be fast, portable, and calorie-dense.

After figuring out that lunchtime on the trail included very little lounging, I started looking closer at what I was eating. Much of my grazing included highly processed foods that wouldn't be a part of my normal diet at home. "But," I rationalized, "It's my reward for hiking hard. Plus, it's not that bad…" But then why did I still feel weird about calling a Snickers bar and a bag of Cheetos "lunch?" I finally listened to my shoulder angel and began experimenting with recipes that provided both caloric density and nutritional density. This is exactly what you'll find in *Trail Grazing*.

# Calories

On a high-power hike, where you'll be pushing your body to its limits and ending each day in an exhausted heap on top of your sleeping bag (too tired to actually crawl *into* your bag), you'll be burning 3,000–4,000 calories. If you're smart, you'll start off with a solid 500+ calorie breakfast and end the day with a rewarding 1,000+ calorie dinner. That means you'll need to consume an additional 1,500–2,500 calories throughout the course of the day. This all happens as you graze, snack, pick, and munch along the way.

"So, all I have to do is eat ten granola bars, and that will satisfy my caloric deficit?" Technically, yes. But realistically, no. When it comes to what to eat while trail grazing, the hungry hiker can either continue to cram the same dry granola bar, mile after mile, hike after hike; or, with a vision that challenges convention, the emboldened hiker can seize new culinary opportunities, and while holding a crumbling commercial granola bar tightly in her trembling fist, boldly declare, "No more!"

But don't blame the commercial granola bar. The truth is that most of us want to get out on the trail with as little fuss as possible. Which is why, I think, so many of us are half-satisfied to grab whatever Ye Old Grocery Mart has on the snack aisle. We know that making something might take a little longer, require a few extra ingredients, and take a bit of kitchen know-how… and maybe that's just a little scary.

However, if you're willing to trust me (and our 50 recipe testers!), I can help you discover a variety of new, quick, easy, and fun foods to take with you on the trail! You can create trail-worthy snacks that are less expensive than store bought bars and snacks, more flavorful (because *you* have control over what goes in), and nutritionally superior to anything processed in a factory. Many of the recipes in *Trail Grazing* come together in a matter of minutes, with just a handful taking some extra time to dehydrate or bake. Many of the recipes are small-batch, which means you can try something new, and it'll be gone before you tire of it. All of the recipes include nutritional powerhouses: whole grains, fruits, vegetables, seeds, nuts, and herbs. And <u>all</u> of the recipes have been trail-tested!

# Getting Started

Now is a good time to browse through the recipes. And by "browse through the recipes," I mean look at the pretty pictures. Really. Decide what *looks* good and bookmark it. Your stomach won't lie.

Once you've decided what to make, read through the recipe at least twice to make sure you understand the ingredient list and method. We're keeping it simple, but a quick read-through will prevent those "oopsie" moments. (And if you do experience an oopsie, many of the recipes are incredibly forgiving.)

Some of the recipes in *Trail Grazing* have ingredients that require a trip to the store, but no ingredient is so weird or obscure that you'd have to cross the county line to find it. Again, we like to keep things simple. You'll find that a lot of the ingredients in *Trail Grazing* appear more than once throughout the recipes, and you probably have many of the ingredients on hand.

After you've tried a recipe, add your own personal notes to it. Many of the recipes in *Trail Grazing* are simple—and for good reason. A simple recipe allows *you* to be the creative one. You get to decide if you want to add sunflower seeds or dried mango to your Go-To Granola Bars (p. 18). You get to decide if your Plantain Chips (p. 56) are feeling spicy or salty. And you get to make the final call on the seasoning for the Hand-Rubbed Artisan Cheese (p. 66).

# What You'll Need

## High-speed Blender or Food Processor

Many of the recipes in this book (particularly the bar recipes) rely on the power of a high-speed blender or food processor to get the ingredients to a fine, smooth consistency. What did folks do before such modern contraptions existed? Well, they probably used a mortar and pestle to pound the tar out of whatever they were making. And perhaps, if they were advanced enough to have a knife, they could chop-chop-chop for hours until the desired consistency was reached. High-speed blenders and food processors speed up the process.

## 8×8-inch Baking Dish

Most of the bars in this book are designed for an 8x8-inch baking dish. Two of the recipes can be made by putting the whole baking dish in the microwave, which is why I suggest using a glass baking dish. If you have a metal baking dish, you can always cook those bars in the oven.

## 8×4-inch Medium Loaf Pan

This little pan is traditionally used for baking bread (Vollkornbrot Whole Rye Bread, p. 59; Fruit and Nut Crostini, p. 60), but it also does a great job of making small batches of granola bars.

## One-quart Microwave-safe Bowl

I use a Pyrex 4-cup glass measuring cup as my microwave-safe bowl. Anything that can hold 4 or more cups of ingredients (and is microwave safe!) should be fine.

## Silicone Spatula

This kitchen tool allows you to scrape all the dreamy goodness out of your bowl and into the pan.

## Parchment Paper

Nearly every recipe in *Trail Grazing* uses parchment paper. Parchment makes it easy to remove bars from baking pans and fruit leather from dehydrators, and it simplifies clean up. Nothing works quite like parchment paper, and you'll be glad you have a roll on hand. I buy my parchment paper from the local restaurant supply store, but most grocery stores stock it as well.

## Chef's Knife

I know you want to use your Swiss Army knife to cut up the Mini Chia Bars (p. 23), but it will be much faster if you use a chef's knife. Save your SAK for snitching little tastes of Hand-Rubbed Artisan Cheese (p. 66) while sitting on a boulder with a view.

## Half-sheet Pan

A half-sheet pan measures 18×13×¾ inches and can be used to make Brownie Bark (p. 27). If you don't have a dehydrator, you can also use it to make any of the fruit leather or jerky recipes by setting your half-sheet pan in the oven at the lowest temperature setting with the oven door cracked.

## Dehydrator

Dehydrating is an ancient method of food preservation. In fact, it's so old that people were dehydrating even before dehydrators were invented! Modern technology speeds up the dehydrating process with electric dehydrators, which circulate warm air and provide adequate ventilation for a low humidity environment.

Electric dehydrators are the most efficient way to dehydrate food (beating out ovens, which can take two to three times longer than a dehydrator).

## Microwave Oven

When I started experimenting with what a microwave could do, I was astonished. Your microwave helps make the glue that holds the Perfect Crunchy Granola Bars (p. 19) together, it delivers fresh Blueberry Muffins (p. 63) in about 2 minutes, it bakes the world's crispiest Flax Crackers (p. 57) and Veggie Crackers (p. 58), it turns pumpkin guts into delectable Roasted Squash Seeds (p. 40)—and it does it all (without preheating) in a fraction of the time of a conventional oven!

Most microwaves run at about 600–1,200 watts. The recipes in *Trail Grazing* were developed and tested using a 1,000-watt microwave. This means that if your microwave has a higher or lower wattage, you may have to do a little trial and error for the microwave recipes—but they shouldn't be off by too much. It also helps if your microwave has a built-in turntable to prevent hotspots in the food.

# Keeping and Storing Your Snacks

Once you've made your trail snacks, you'll want to package them up and label them. There are several options for packaging, and each has its pros and cons.

**Zip Top Bags**
- Pro: cheap, waterproof, reusable, transparent, good for loose snacks like nuts and crackers
- Con: can't be composted

**Plastic Wrap**
- Pro: cheap, transparent, great for packaging bars
- Con: can't be composted

**Plastic Storage Containers**
- Pro: lightweight, watertight, airtight, store multiple snacks
- Con: bulky

**Parchment Paper**
- Pro: lightweight, sturdy, compostable
- Con: not transparent, more expensive than plastic wrap, not airtight

**Waxed Paper**
- Pro: inexpensive, makes great tinder
- Con: not airtight, not durable

**Glass Mason Jars**
- Pro: great for long-term food storage, does a nice job of keeping crackers crisp
- Con: heavy, breakable, can't come with you on the trail

**Aluminum Foil**
- Pro: wraps snacks securely
- Con: opaque, expensive, used foil not recyclable

**Beeswax Wrap (a waxed-cotton plastic wrap alternative)**
- Pro: reusable, durable, compostable, fun designs
- Con: not airtight or watertight, kinda pricy

# How Long Will My Snacks Last?

We've tested each of the recipes to last at least five to seven days at room temperature. "But," we hear you say, "hikes aren't at 'room temperature!'" You're right. Every hike is different and temperatures can sometimes fluctuate wildly from freezing to scorching—all on the same hike! A recipe that lasts for a week in the kitchen may not have the same staying power on your trip of four days at 90 degrees.

And what about food safety for perishables? Food safety experts will tell you that some foods should never be at room temperature longer than two hours. And they're right. The risk for foodborne illness increases the longer your cheese is stuffed in your back pocket. So to comply with the folks in suits, we should probably tell you that your Hand-Rubbed Artisan Cheese (p. 66) and "Everything Bagel" Mozzarella Cheese Sticks (p. 67) need to be consumed within the first mile of hiking. (And, this is where a little of that hiker's intuition needs to come into play. Decide what your rules for food safety are on the trail, and don't tell the folks in suits.)

One more note: clean hands go a long way toward preventing foodborne illness on the trail. Wash your hands before eating, or simply eat directly from the bag, horse style.

# Final Words

Many of the recipes in *Trail Grazing* are calorie-dense, which means they're *not* food for folks training for a Netflix marathon. These foods are designed to fuel your real-world, muddy-boots, sweaty-pits, gritty-necked adventures. These are *power-filled* foods that will awaken your senses, inspire your mind, and nourish your body, every step of the trail.

# Bars + Bites

Three things scare me: Hitchcock's *North By Northwest*, suburban Tupperware parties, and recipes with looooong ingredient lists. This cookbook has no crop duster chase scenes, no high-pressure plastic kitchenware sales, and I've really tried to keep the ingredient lists short—and this especially includes the bar recipes. Brief is good. And I think we're all grown up enough to know that even if a recipe doesn't call for a handful of sunflower seeds, you can throw some in without tipping the balance.

If you're like me, there's a good chance that you'll find a bar recipe in this chapter that you adore, and glom onto it like I did with the Go-To Granola Bars (p. 18). You'll find your favorite add-ins and have a special way you cut and wrap the bars each time. It'll be your little pre-trail ritual. Once you have your ritual down, you'll be that much closer to getting out the door.

Cutting the bars is fairly simple. If it's an 8×8-inch pan of bars, I typically cut right down the middle so that there are two 8×4-inch rectangles (or two really huuuge granola bars!). Then, I cut the 8×4-inch rectangles into whatever width of bar I want. Usually I go for about 1½–2 inches per bar, which gets me 8–12 bars per 8×8-inch pan (or 4–6 bars per 8×4-inch pan). You can also ditch the bar idea altogether and cut the pan into 1×1-inch bite-sized pieces.

# Go-To Granola Bars

*This is the granola bar recipe I keep coming back to. It's so simple.*

*Makes an 8×8-inch pan of bars*
*2,592 calories*
*114 calories/ounce*

**Ingredients**
2 cups oats
1 cup crisp rice cereal
½ cup peanut butter
½ cup honey

This is a very basic recipe. If you're wondering where all the "goodies" and "mix-ins" are, they are living in the land of your imagination. Throw in up to a cup of whatever sounds good.

Measure oats and crisp rice cereal into a large bowl and set aside.

Measure peanut butter and honey in a one-quart microwave-safe bowl and stir to combine. Heat in a microwave for 2 minutes.

Pour the peanut butter and honey mixture over the oat mixture. Stir well until everything is evenly coated.

Spread mixture evenly into a parchment-lined 8×8-inch baking dish. With another piece of parchment paper and a hot pad, press down firmly and evenly. If you have a second 8×8-inch baking dish, you can press that on top of the granola bars to make the bars even more compact.

When cooled, slice into bars and wrap individually. Store wrapped bars in an airtight container.

# Perfect Crunchy Granola Bars

*You would not believe how many attempts it took to create this recipe for the perfect crunchy granola bar. I made lots of almost crunchy granola bars in the process, and a few sad batches of limp and syrupy bars, too. This is a no-fail recipe.*

*Makes an 8×8-inch pan of bars*
*969 calories*
*102 calories/ounce*

**Ingredients**

1 cup oats
1 cup crisp rice cereal
¼ cup honey
¼ teaspoon salt

This granola bar is full of crunch in all the right places, but if you want to 10× the crunch and the flavor, throw in a handful of toasted chopped almonds when you mix the ingredients.

Mix all ingredients in a one-quart microwave-safe bowl.

Microwave for 1 minute, then stir. Continue to microwave in 30-second increments, stirring each time, until mixture begins to brown but not burn. Cooking time will vary by microwave, but it should take about 3 minutes total.

Spread mixture evenly into a parchment-lined 8×8-inch baking dish. With another piece of parchment paper and a hot pad, press down firmly and evenly. If you have a second 8×8-inch baking dish, you can press that on top of the granola bars to make the bars even more compact.

Cut bars while they're still warm (but not hot), then let cool completely.

Wrap individually and store in an airtight container.

# Fruit + Nut Bars

*These delightful bars require no baking and just a few minutes of work. The ingredients aren't just in the recipe title—they are the recipe title!*

Makes an 8×4-inch pan of bars
943–1,178 calories
116 calories/ounce

**Ingredients**

**Date + Almond Bar**

1 cup dates

1 cup almonds

**Apricot + Cashew + Coconut Bar**

1 cup apricots

1 cup cashews

2 tablespoons unsweetened shredded coconut

**Cherry + Dark Chocolate + Pecan Bar**

1 cup dried cherries

1 cup pecans

2 tablespoons cocoa powder

2 tablespoons chocolate chips (optional)

Add ingredients to blender or food processor. Pulse until very finely chopped and mixture holds together. This is an important step—make sure the mixture holds together when pressed, or your bars will fall apart.

Press fruit and nut mixture firmly into a parchment-lined 8×4-inch medium loaf pan and refrigerate until firm.

Wrap individually and store in an airtight container.

You're welcome to add a pinch of salt or even cinnamon to any of the fruit and nut bars to bring out their natural flavors, but be careful about adding too many "add-ins." There's something satisfying about a recipe that has only two or three ingredients. Don't muddle it up with complexity!

# Quick Chocolate Caramel Bars

*These bars probably share more DNA with your favorite candy bar than they do with a granola bar. However there are some advantages to this bar that a Snicke—oops!—that other bars don't have. It won't melt in your pack, it's got a huge pile of whole grains mixed in, and you can add whatever mix-ins you want. I'm adding a handful of toasted hazelnuts to my next batch.*

*Makes an 8×8-inch pan of bars*
*1,695 calories*
*113 calories/ounce*

### Ingredients

1½ cups oats
1 cup crisp rice cereal
½ cup brown sugar
¼ cup butter
¼ cup honey
¼ cup cocoa powder
½ teaspoon salt
½ teaspoon vanilla

In a medium bowl, mix together the oats and crisp rice cereal.

In a quart microwave-safe mixing bowl, combine brown sugar, butter, honey, cocoa powder, salt, and vanilla. Microwave for 1 minute, then stir. Microwave for another 2 minutes. Add the chocolate caramel mixture to the oats and crisp rice cereal, and stir until evenly coated.

Press mixture firmly into a parchment-lined 8×8-inch baking dish. Place in the fridge for 10 minutes until firm.

Cut, wrap individually, and store in an airtight container.

# Naturally Sweet + Chewy Baked Bars

*The sweetness in the recipe comes from the dimples in your cheeks and the little birdies that fly into your kitchen and tie your apron strings while you whistle a happy tune. It also comes from the dried fruit, milk powder, and drizzle of honey.*

Makes an 8×8-inch pan of bars
2,025 calories
103 calories/ounce

**Ingredients**

1 cup oats
1 cup almonds
1 cup raisins (or any dried fruit)
2 tablespoons NIDO whole milk powder
½ teaspoon cinnamon
½ teaspoon salt
2 tablespoons honey
1 egg

You can also bake these bars in the oven. Preheat the oven to 350°F. Bake for 20 minutes. Cool and cut into bars.

Add dry ingredients to a blender or food processor. Pulse until all ingredients are roughly the same size, with a grainy texture.

Add honey and egg to mixture and continue to pulse until all ingredients are incorporated. You may need to scrape down the sides a few times to fully incorporate all ingredients.

When everything is mixed, scrape mixture into a parchment-lined 8×8-inch baking dish. The mixture will be thick and sticky.

Smooth out the mixture as much as you can, then bake in a microwave for 2 minutes. Remove from microwave and check for any spots that appear undercooked. Return to microwave for 30-second intervals and continue cooking until the mixture has firmed up and there are no wet or uncooked spots.

Let bars cool completely before cutting. Wrap individually and store in an airtight container.

# Mini Chia Bars

*Once I climbed a mountain, carrying only a Mini Chia Bar. I hiked for days. When I reached the peak, I met a wise man in a hut. He looked at my chia bar, then looked at me and said, "A little chia goes a long way." I turned around and climbed back down.*

Makes an 8×4-inch pan of bars
1,579 calories
110 calories/ounce

**Ingredients**
1 cup dried figs, stems removed
¼ cup chia seeds
¼ cup cocoa powder
¼ cup unsweetened shredded coconut
¼ cup oats
¼ cup chocolate chips

Add all ingredients to a blender or food processor and pulse 1–2 minutes until mixture holds together when pinched. Scrape down sides as needed.

Firmly press the mixture into a parchment-lined 8×4-inch medium loaf pan. Place in the refrigerator until firm.

Cut into mini bars and store in an airtight container.

> Next time you climb a mountain, bring an extra Mini Chia Bar for the wise man in the hut.

# "Thoughtful" Bars

*I wanted to call these "Kind Bars," but that name's already taken. And besides, these "Thoughtful" Bars aren't just kind, they also open the car door for you, never forget your anniversary, and side with you when your mother-in-law criticizes your paint color choice in the dining room.*

Makes an 8×8-inch pan of bars
2,053 calories
141 calories/ounce

### Ingredients

1 cup almonds, roughly chopped
1 cup peanuts
¼ cup honey
½ teaspoon salt
½ cup crisp rice cereal
½ cup chocolate chips (for drizzle topping)

Line an 8×8-inch baking dish with parchment paper.

In a one-quart microwave-safe bowl, mix almonds, peanuts, honey, and salt. Microwave for 4 minutes, stirring every minute.

Remove nut and honey mixture from microwave and add crisp rice cereal. Mix well. Pour mixture into the parchment-lined 8x8 baking dish. Using another piece of parchment paper and a hot pad, press mixture down until it's compact. Mixture will be extremely hot, so take care not to burn yourself.

Slice while bars are warm but not hot. Cool completely, then wrap individually and store in an airtight container.

If you want to drizzle chocolate on top of bars, cut the bars, then put ½ cup chocolate chips into a small microwave-safe bowl. Microwave at 15-second increments, stirring each time, until chips are mostly melted. Transfer melted chocolate into a zip top sandwich bag, snip off the tip of the corner, and drizzle in a zigzag pattern on bars. Place bars in refrigerator and wrap individually after chocolate hardens.

# Big Batch Lunch Lady Bars

*Sometimes you're planning a hike with lots of people who will be lots of hungry, and they want lots of food. This is a lunchtime classic that not only packs well but will keep your hungry hikers happy on the uphills and down.*

*Makes an 18×13-inch pan of bars*
*5,527 calories*
*124 calories/ounce*

**Ingredients**

4 cups oats
1½ cups sugar
1 cup peanut butter
½ cup butter
2 eggs
1 teaspoon salt
½ teaspoon baking soda
1 cup chocolate chips

You don't need to grease or line the cookie sheet. There is enough butter in these bars to grease themselves right through the gates of heaven.

Preheat oven to 350°F.

Put all ingredients, except chocolate chips, into a large mixing bowl and mix well.

Spread mixture onto a 18×13-inch half-sheet pan, using your hands to flatten the dough evenly into the pan.

Bake for 25 minutes, or until golden brown on edges.

After baking, sprinkle chocolate chips on top. When the chocolate has melted, spread it evenly using a spatula.

Cool completely, and slice into squares or bars.

Wrap individually and store in an airtight container.

# Black Bean Brownies

*These brownies have black beans and chocolate—an unlikely but inspired combination. Warning: feeding these brownies to people you love without disclosing the fact that there are beans in them may cause trust issues. Proceed with caution.*

*Makes an 8×8-inch pan of bars*

*2,167 calories*

*76 calories/ounce*

**Ingredients**

1 can (15 ounces) black beans, rinsed and drained (or 1½ cups cooked black beans)

1 cup dates

½ cup oats

½ cup water

¼ cup cocoa powder

2 teaspoons vanilla

1 teaspoon baking powder

1 cup chocolate chips

½ cup chocolate chips (for topping)

Add all ingredients, except chocolate chips, into a blender or food processor. Blend until all ingredients are pureed. Add 1 cup chocolate chips and pulse 2–3 times until chips are incorporated. Then spread brownie batter in a parchment-lined microwave-safe 8×8-inch baking dish.

Microwave for 4 minutes 30 seconds.

Sprinkle ½ cup chocolate chips on top and wait for them to melt. Carefully spread melted chocolate on top of brownies and let brownies cool completely before cutting.

Wrap individually and store in an airtight container.

> These brownies can be baked in the oven instead of the microwave. Bake at 350°F for 15–18 minutes.

# Brownie Bark

*So many of the foods that go into a hiker's pack end up smooshed to bits. Well, here's a treat that is not only meant to be broken, smooshed, and cracked, but tastes even better when it's got those craggy uneven edges.*

*Makes an 18×13-inch pan of brownie bark*
*1,058 calories*
*119 calories/ounce*

### Ingredients

½ cup whole wheat flour
½ cup sugar
¼ cup cocoa powder
¼ teaspoon baking soda
¼ teaspoon salt
2 eggs
2 tablespoons oil
1 teaspoon vanilla

Preheat oven to 350°F.

Line an 18×13-inch half-sheet pan with parchment paper.

In a medium bowl, mix whole wheat flour, sugar, cocoa powder, baking soda, and salt. Add eggs, oil, and vanilla. Stir until a smooth batter forms. Spread batter onto parchment-lined baking sheet into an approximately 16×11-inch rectangle, leaving a 1-inch margin on all sides.

Bake 20 minutes.

Remove from oven and cut or break into bite-sized pieces with a pizza cutter or large knife. Turn off oven and return pan to oven for 10–15 minutes to further dry out the brownie bark.

Brownie bark will crisp as it cools.

Store in an airtight container.

---

I don't really have anything to say here. I just got used to writing a note at the end of each recipe and I missed our time together. Glad we could have this moment. Thanks.

# Whole Food Truffles

*My mom made these all the time when I was a kid. And by "all the time," I mean probably twice. I think she originally found the recipe, or something like it, in Mother Earth News. It's simple and can be made with the kids or by the kids.*

Makes 20 1-inch balls
1,186 calories
119 calories/ounce

**Ingredients**

1 cup almonds
1 cup raisins
¼ cup sesame seeds or unsweetened shredded coconut

You can also roll the balls in oat flour or chia seeds.

Put almonds and raisins in a blender or food processor and pulse until the mixture starts to hold together without falling apart.

Put raisin and almond mixture on a cutting board and divide into 20 pieces. Roll pieces into 1-inch balls.

Put several balls at a time into a small bowl with sesame seeds or coconut and roll until completely coated. Coat the rest of the balls, a few at a time.

Store balls in airtight container.

# Hikers' Taffy

*If you like to share snacks while hiking, these treats are individually wrapped and 100 percent sharable.*

*Makes 12 pieces*
*534 calories*
*116 calories/ounce*

**Ingredients**
½ cup oats
¼ cup NIDO whole milk powder
2 tablespoons honey
1 tablespoon peanut butter

This is a great recipe to get creative with! Feel free to add mini chocolate chips, finely-chopped dried blueberries, or a dash of cinnamon.

Cut 12 pieces of 5×5-inch parchment paper.

Blend oats to a fine powder in a blender or food processor.

Combine the oat powder and the rest of the ingredients in a medium bowl. Mix well. Mixture should be thick and taffy-like.

Divide mixture into 12 equal portions. Roll each portion into a small log and wrap with a piece of 5×5-inch parchment paper.

Store in an airtight container.

# Fruit Leather

Fruit leather is a trail favorite. It provides micronutrients, fiber, and a burst of sweetness. There's a good reason to make it yourself instead of going for the commercially made fruit leather: ingredient control. When you make it yourself, you know exactly what went into the fruit leather and what you're going to get out of it.

Commercial fruit leather has benefited far too long from the "halo effect." A typical box of commercial fruit leather has pictures of fruit, which leads the gentle consumer to believe that it's a virtuous, nutritious product. But in 2011, the Center for Science in the Public Interest caught on to the deceptive tactics of food manufacturers, noting that commercial fruit leather had more in common with gummy bears than with an apple.

Looking for another reason to make your own fruit leather? When you make your own, you don't have to limit the ingredients to just fruit. (Gasp!) There's no reason why we can't combine fruits and vegetables into one sweet delicious bit of trail snacking. (Double gasp!) Sorry to spring such a revolutionary idea on you without warning. Yes, fruits and vegetables. Together. In fruit leather. Be a rabble-rouser.

By the way, here are some common ingredients in commercial fruit leather that I've chosen not to include in my fruit leather recipes: corn syrup, polydextrose, dried corn syrup, sugar, maltodextrin, palm oil, sodium citrate, monoglycerides, malic acid, dextrose, acetylated monoglycerides, and artificial color (yellow 5, blue 1, and red 40).

# Simple Fruit Leather

*Think of this recipe as a canvas for your other imaginative variations on fruit leather. You could add fresh nectarines next time, or mangoes, or a handful of frozen blueberries. The whole point is that fruit leather is whatever flavor you want it to be! But with this recipe, let's start simple.*

Makes 2 servings
400 calories
78 calories/ounce

**Ingredients**
2 apples, cored and quartered
2 bananas

Put ingredients into a blender or food processor and puree until smooth.

Pour onto parchment-lined dehydrator trays so that the puree is about 1/8–1/4 inch thick. The thinner it's spread, the shorter the drying time. The thicker it's spread, the longer the drying time. Simple math for simple fruit leather.

After 2–3 hours, check on your fruit leather. You want it to be pliable and slightly sticky. You should be able to pull the edge away from the parchment paper. If it's gummy or wet, let it continue to dehydrate. Check every hour or so.

Cut into strips and store in an airtight container.

In my freezer, I keep a container of random fruit that I want to add to my next batch of fruit leather. What goes into the container? Overripe bananas, a peach that wasn't as sweet as I hoped it would be, the core from a pineapple (try it!), coconut pulp left over from making coconut milk, and a few slices of apple left over from lunch. It helps avoid food waste and makes our fruit leather interesting.

**Troubleshooting**

If you left your fruit leather in the dehydrator too long and it got crispy, there are ways to fix that.

A. Place the fruit leather in the high-humidity produce drawer in your refrigerator for several hours. That will soften the fruit leather just enough so that you'll be able to cut it into strips without it cracking.

B. Place a wet paper towel in your microwave, and set the parchment paper with fruit leather on top. Microwave for 30 seconds and leave in microwave for several minutes for the fruit leather to absorb the humidity.

C. Enjoy the crispy fruit leather. It's like potato chips made of fruit!

# Berry + Beet Fruit Leather

*If you're ready to up your fruit leather game, then the bold next step is to add a companion vegetable. For this recipe, the natural veggie paring for berries is beets! Both berries and beets are saturated in color, loaded with nutrients, and killin' it in the fiber department.*

Makes 4 servings
833 calories
97 calories/ounce

**Ingredients**

2 cups mixed berries (frozen)
4 bananas
¼ cup canned beets, drained, or ¼-cup-size fresh beet, raw
¼ cup honey (optional)

Honey not only gives fruit leather a magazine-cover shine, but it also compensates for what vegetables lack in sweetness. Feel free to give the fruit and veggie puree a taste test before deciding whether or not to add the honey. You make the call.

Put all ingredients into a blender or food processor and puree until smooth. You may need to scrape down the sides a few times to make sure all the ingredients are incorporated.

Pour onto parchment-lined dehydrator trays so that the puree is about ⅛–¼ inch thick. The thinner it's spread, the shorter the drying time. The thicker it's spread, the longer the drying time.

After 2–3 hours, check on your fruit leather. You want it to be pliable and slightly sticky. You should be able to pull the edge away from the parchment paper. If it's gummy or wet, let it continue to dehydrate. Check every hour or so.

Cut into strips and store in an airtight container.

# Vanilla Orange Fruit Leather

*This recipe has a huge dose of Vitamin C—found not only in the fruit of the orange, but in the pith and peel, too (which are great sources of fiber as well)!*

*Makes 4 servings*
*802 calories*
*91 calories/ounce*

**Ingredients**

1 medium orange (with peel)
2 carrots
4 bananas
¼ cup honey
1 tablespoon vanilla

There's no need to remove the fruit leather from the parchment paper before you cut it into strips.

Put all ingredients into a blender or food processor and puree until smooth. You may need to scrape down the sides a few times to make sure all the ingredients are incorporated.

Pour onto parchment-lined dehydrator trays so that the puree is about ⅛–¼ inch thick. The thinner it's spread, the shorter the drying time. The thicker it's spread, the longer the drying time.

After 2–3 hours, check on your fruit leather. You want it to be pliable and slightly sticky. You should be able to pull the edge away from the parchment paper. If it's gummy or wet, let it continue to dehydrate. Check every hour or so.

Cut into strips and store in an airtight container.

# Cucumber + Lime Fruit Leather

*It might seem weird to put a cucumber into fruit leather, but it's no stranger than hiking up a hill with a 30-pound pack on your back—for fun. The lime in this recipe is used whole, which adds all the flavor of lime, along with its sharp, somewhat bitter notes. And do add the fresh mint if you can. This recipe is for the adventurous palate.*

*Makes 4 servings*
*743 calories*
*93 calories/ounce*

**Ingredients**
1 cucumber
1 lime (not peeled)
4 bananas
¼ cup honey
¼ cup fresh mint (optional)

Roughly chop cucumber and lime and add to blender. Add the rest of the ingredients to a blender or food processor. Puree until smooth.

Pour onto parchment-lined dehydrator trays so that the puree is about ⅛–¼ inch thick. The thinner it's spread, the shorter the drying time. The thicker it's spread, the longer the drying time.

After 2–3 hours, check on your fruit leather. You want it to be pliable and slightly sticky. You should be able to pull the edge away from the parchment paper. If it's gummy or wet, let it continue to dehydrate. Check every hour or so.

Cut into strips and store in an airtight container.

# Yogurt Fruit Leather

*OK, let's play "Two Truths and a Lie:"*
   *A. Yogurt Fruit Leather is super sweet and creamy.*
   *B. Yogurt Fruit Leather has a fun taffy-like chewy texture.*
   *C. Yogurt Fruit Leather looks so incredibly edible with no weird streaky-lookin' stuff going on that makes it look like a cut of fatty pork belly.*
*Now that you know the truth, I say, make it anyway. Ugly is nothing to be ashamed of.*

*Makes 4 servings*
*896 calories*
*93 calories/ounce*

**Ingredients**
32-ounce container fruit-flavored yogurt (any flavor)

Any flavor or variety of yogurt (soy, coconut, etc.) works in this recipe.

Stir yogurt in container so that it's smooth and spreadable. Spread yogurt smoothly and evenly (1/8–1/4 inch thick) onto a parchment-lined dehydrator tray.

Dehydrating times vary, although most dehydrators will take 3–5 hours. Be careful not to over-dry, or it will become brittle (a.k.a. Crunchy Yogurt Chips).

Remove from dehydrator and cut into strips. Store in an airtight container.

# Nuts + Seeds

Nuts and seeds are calorically dense, nutritionally packed, convenient, flavorful snacks. Is it possible to improve on something that's nearly perfect? Yep.

We scientifically scanned thousands of flavor profiles using a very large IBM 7090 mainframe. And with the help of our intern, Donny the Gerbil, we discovered the perfect mix of sweet, salty, smoky, and spicy. You now have access to never-before-seen recipes that have been approved by Marvin and Donny, the computer and the gerbil, respectively.

(The actual truth is, Donny approved of every single recipe without reservation, but Marvin was less than enthusiastic about the Black Bean "Nuts," his reason being, "0111010101101000." As if *that's* a valid response.)

One of the things that I love about this section is that nearly all of the recipes take only minutes to make, meaning you're ready to blaze a trail with a high-powered snack faster than it takes to fold up a topographic map. Correctly.

# Roasted Squash Seeds

*There are so many great things about roasted squash seeds! First, they are incredibly nutritious. Second, they are undeniably delicious! Third, most people throw them out—which puts squash seeds in the new and trendy category of "edible food waste." But what I love most about this recipe is that it takes just minutes to roast these seeds to perfection in your microwave.*

Makes ½ cup of seeds
143 calories
126 calories/ounce

**Ingredients**

½ cup seeds from any winter squash (butternut, pumpkin, acorn squash, delicata, etc.)
¼ teaspoon salt

Sometimes I cook a whole squash (without removing the seeds) in my electric pressure cooker. Those seeds can also be roasted in the microwave; however, you will need to adjust the cooking time and watch them carefully, as they brown quickly and get very crispy.

Remove seeds from your squash. They will be slimy and stringy—but don't let that stop you! Put the seeds in a colander and rinse them and remove the stringy stuff. Shake the colander to remove excess water.

Add seeds to a one-quart microwave-safe bowl. Sprinkle seeds with salt.

Microwave 1 minute. Stir. Then continue to cook in 30-second increments, stirring each time, until seeds are the desired crispness. You may hear popping sounds toward the end of cooking, depending on which type of seed you use. You may even see some of the seeds begin to brown.

# Coconut + Curry Cashews

*Coconut, curry, and cashews. A triple threat. These nuts are going to be one of your favorite snacks on and off the trail. We played it safe with this recipe and were conservative with the curry powder to please the masses. Feel free to double or triple the amount of curry (and pepper) to suit your taste.*

*Makes 1 cup of nuts*
*883 calories*
*150 calories/ounce*

**Ingredients**

1 cup cashews, unsalted (raw or toasted)
2 tablespoons unsweetened shredded coconut
1 tablespoon honey
½ teaspoon salt
¼ teaspoon ground black pepper
¼ teaspoon curry powder

Mix all ingredients in a one-quart microwave-safe bowl.

Microwave for 2–3 minutes, stirring every 30 seconds. When mixture starts to brown, remove from microwave and spread on a piece of parchment paper to cool.

Store in an airtight container.

If you use salted cashews, omit salt from the recipe.

# Smoky Maple BBQ Nuts

*I love smoked food. These nuts just fill a hole in my heart that only smoked food can fill. The flavor in this recipe relies on a little bottle of what I call "backpacker's perfume." Liquid smoke is the secret to getting that intense smokehouse flavor. Liquid smoke is made by burning hardwoods (hickory, mesquite, etc.) in a chamber, then capturing the condensation from the cooled smoke.*

*Makes 1 cup of nuts*
*957 calories*
*152 calories/ounce*

**Ingredients**

1 cup mixed nuts, unsalted
1 tablespoon maple syrup
1 teaspoon barbeque sauce or tomato paste
1 teaspoon liquid smoke
½ teaspoon salt
½ teaspoon ground black pepper

Mix all ingredients in a one-quart microwave-safe bowl.

Microwave for 2-3 minutes, stirring every 30 seconds. Watch carefully to avoid burning.

Remove immediately from bowl and spread onto a piece of parchment paper. Nuts will harden upon cooling.

Store in an airtight container.

> Try to find a grocery store that sells nuts in bulk. Not only can you get the exact amount you need, but you can create your own unique blend of mixed nuts.

# Sesame Ginger Pecans

*This recipe is what Bob Ross would call a "happy accident." All the ingredients just kind of came together, and the flavors played nicely on the kitchen playground. If you love ginger, go ahead and double the amount. You can also use this particular nut mix at home as a topping on Asian salads. Yerrrrr welcome.*

*Makes 1 cup of nuts*
*838 calories*
*178 calories/ounce*

### Ingredients

1 cup pecans
1 tablespoon sesame seeds
1 tablespoon honey
1 teaspoon salt
1 teaspoon fresh grated ginger or ½ teaspoon ground ginger
1 teaspoon sesame oil

Mix all ingredients in a one-quart microwave-safe bowl.

Microwave for 2–3 minutes, stirring every 30 seconds. Watch carefully to avoid burning.

Remove immediately from bowl and spread onto a piece of parchment paper. Nuts will harden upon cooling.

Store in an airtight container.

# Black Bean "Nuts"

Everyone thinks nuts are sooo great, and they are! But it's fun to find that satisfying crunch other places within the vegetable kingdom. Black beans that have been cooked and quickly dehydrated in the oven will give you that satisfying crunch, along with a boatload of fiber and respect.

Makes ¾ cup of "nuts"
381 calories
100 calories/ounce

**Ingredients**

1 can (15 ounces) black beans, rinsed and drained (or 1½ cups cooked black beans)
1 teaspoon oil
½ teaspoon salt

Preheat oven to 400 degrees Fahrenheit.

Spread beans on a parchment-lined baking sheet, making sure they are evenly spread out. Do <u>not</u> add oil and salt yet.

Bake for 20 minutes in oven. Remove beans from oven and stir. Return beans to oven for an extra 5–10 minutes to finish drying out completely. When beans are dried and crunchy, remove from oven.

When nuts are still warm, season with oil and salt.

Black Bean "Nuts" are a healthful, satisfying snack, and they are also a multi-use snack! Anything you don't eat while trail grazing can be stirred into dinner. The beans will rehydrate and provide variety of texture and color within your meal.

# Cocoa Dusted Almonds

*Cocoa Dusted Almonds are the kind of fancy snack you spend $9.50 for in an airport gift shop. And if you've ever had a layover in a city with less-than-stellar airport food options, you know they're totally worth it. However, if you lean in close, I'll whisper a secret: you can make Cocoa Dusted Almonds at home… and it takes only minutes.*

*Makes 1 cup of nuts*
*599 calories*
*135 calories/ounce*

**Ingredients**
½ cup almonds, roasted
¼ cup chocolate chips
¼ cup cocoa powder
¼ teaspoon salt

Heat almonds and chocolate chips in microwave for 30 seconds. Stir. Heat for another 15–20 seconds until chocolate is mostly melted.

Add cocoa powder and salt to almond mixture and stir until almonds are coated. Spread evenly on a piece of parchment paper and let cool. When cooled, store in an airtight container.

> If you have raw almonds and want to roast them quickly, you can microwave them for 2–3 minutes, checking every 30 seconds and giving them a quick stir. Be careful, though. Don't let them burn!

# Montezuma's Chocolate Drops

*These little chocolate drops are made from unsweetened chocolate and get their sweetness from the raisins. They get their crunch from the nuts and chia seeds. And they get their cinnamon from a little jar I keep in my cupboard labeled "cinnamon."*

*Makes 12 small candies*
*370 calories*
*144 calories/ounce*

**Ingredients**

1 ounce unsweetened Baker's chocolate, finely diced
2 tablespoons raisins
2 tablespoons peanuts
2 teaspoons chia seeds
½ teaspoon cinnamon

Heat chocolate in several 15-second increments in microwave in a small microwave-safe bowl, stirring each time until chocolate is mostly melted. Remove from microwave and continue to stir until chocolate is fully melted.

Add remaining ingredients, and stir until everything is coated in chocolate.

Using a small spoon, scoop ½-teaspoon drops of chocolate mixture and place on a parchment-lined plate. Let cool in the refrigerator.

Store in an airtight container.

These will melt on hot hikes. They will also melt on cold hikes if you keep them in your pants pocket. They will melt by the dying embers of an evening fire. They will also melt on the dashboard of your car at the trailhead. Melted chocolate isn't bad, it's just messy.

# Whole Food Jerky

Beef jerky is a time-honored trail food which dates back to the 1500s. The Quechua Native American tribe called their smoked and salted llama meat "ch'arki," which is where we got today's word "jerky."

In *Trail Grazing*, we're taking a Modern American spin on jerky by incorporating star players from the plant kingdom into the meat. To do this, you'll need a high-speed blender or a food processor. You'll also need an open mind and an adventurous spirit.

And vegans, have no fear: these recipes can be veganized by substituting a pound of sautéed mushrooms plus a half cup of ground flaxseed per pound of meat (and go easy on the salt!). The mushrooms not only give the vegan jerky that classic jerky toughness, but the sautéing brings crazy amounts of flavor to the party.

# Beef + Veggie Jerky

*Beef + Veggie Jerky is almost a full meal. The only thing it's missing is a sesame seed bun.*

Makes 4 servings
1,387 calories
107 calories/ounce

### Ingredients

1 pound ground beef
2 cups spinach
1 medium onion, diced
1 red bell pepper
½ cup tomato paste
¼ cup honey
1 tablespoon salt
1 tablespoon liquid smoke

Place all ingredients in a blender or food processor. Pulse until ingredients are a smooth paste. You may need to scrape down sides of blender or food processor to ensure all ingredients are incorporated.

Add mixture into a jerky gun and put strips of jerky mixture directly onto dehydrator tray. If you don't have a jerky gun, spread mixture ¼ inch thick on parchment paper that has been cut to fit your dehydrator tray.

Dehydrate for about 5 hours or until the jerky is dried out. (You can speed up the dehydration time by cutting the partially dried jerky into smaller strips, then continuing to dehydrate until fully dried.)

---

One time, we made two batches of beef jerky—one was classic beef jerky, and the other was spiked with super-spicy habanero chili flakes. We dumped both jerkies into the same bag and had fun playing "jerky roulette."

**Variations**

Try adding these ingredients for some fun takes on Beef + Veggie Jerky. Just mix them in with the base recipe.

**Orange Beef Jerky**

1 medium orange (with peel)
2 tablespoons soy sauce
2 teaspoons garlic powder

**Pizza Jerky**

½ cup Parmesan cheese
1 tablespoon Italian seasoning
2 teaspoons garlic powder

**Sweet Thai Chili Jerky**

2 tablespoons red chili flakes
2 teaspoons garlic powder

# California Jerky

When I think of California, I think of quaint roadside fruit stands, bountiful farmers' markets, and exciting culinary trends. California Jerky captures some of the flavors, colors and bounty of the great state of California. The title of this recipe is in no way a cheap jab at Californians' driving abilities.

*Makes 4 servings*
*2,144 calories*
*108 calories/ounce*

**Ingredients**

1 pound ground beef
2 cups kale, washed and stemmed
1 cup dried apricots
1 cup almonds
¼ cup honey
1 tablespoon liquid smoke
1 tablespoon salt

Pulse all ingredients in a blender or food processor until everything is pureed.

Add mixture into a jerky gun and put strips of jerky mixture directly onto dehydrator tray. If you don't have a jerky gun, spread mixture ¼ inch thick on parchment paper that has been cut to fit your dehydrator tray.

Dehydrate for about 5 hours or until the jerky is dried out. (You can speed up the dehydration time by cutting the partially dried jerky into smaller strips, then continuing to dehydrate until fully dried.)

> You might not have liquid smoke in your pantry, but it's worth picking up a bottle. We use it in soups and sauces as well. If you just can't find liquid smoke, Worcestershire sauce might be an acceptable substitute (but cut the salt in the recipe).

# Beef + Bean Burrito Jerky

*This is in my dehydrator right now. I love it because it tastes like a beef and bean burrito. Wrap a tortilla around a stick of this stuff, and you've got a passport to Burritoville.*

*Makes 4 servings*
*1,754 calories*
*102 calories/ounce*

**Ingredients**

1 pound ground beef
1 can (15 ounces) black beans, rinsed and drained (or 1½ cups cooked black beans)
½ cup tomato paste
½ medium onion, diced
¼ cup honey
¼ cup chili powder
1 tablespoon liquid smoke
1 tablespoon salt

Pulse all ingredients in a blender or food processor until everything is pureed.

Add mixture into a jerky gun and put strips of jerky mixture directly onto dehydrator tray. If you don't have a jerky gun, spread mixture ¼ inch thick on parchment paper that has been cut to fit your dehydrator tray.

Dehydrate for about 5 hours or until the jerky is dried out. (You can speed up the dehydration time by cutting the partially dried jerky into smaller strips, then continuing to dehydrate until fully dried.)

This jerky is rehydratable and really *can* be used as a filling for your flour tortillas. Just pour ¼ cup of boiling water over a handful of jerky that's been torn or cut into smaller pieces. Wait 2–3 minutes for mixture to rehydrate. If you're feeling extra "beany," see the recipe for Black Bean "Nuts" (p. 44), and add those to the mix.

# Thanksgiving Turkey Jerky

*Now you can celebrate Thanksgiving all year round. I'm thankful for trees and nature and my family and chocolate and my ukulele and everything.*

Makes 4 servings
2,155 calories
115 calories/ounce

### Ingredients

1 pound ground turkey
1 cup dried cranberries
1 cup sunflower seed kernels, raw, unsalted
1 tablespoon salt
2 teaspoons poultry seasoning
2 teaspoons liquid smoke

Pulse cranberry and sunflower seeds in a blender or food processor until roughly chopped. Add ground turkey, salt, poultry seasoning, and liquid smoke and continue to pulse until everything is combined.

Add mixture into a jerky gun and put strips of jerky mixture directly onto dehydrator tray. If you don't have a jerky gun, spread mixture ¼ inch thick on parchment paper that has been cut to fit tray.

Dehydrate for about 5 hours or until the jerky is dried out. (You can speed up the dehydration time by cutting the partially dried jerky into smaller strips, then continuing to dehydrate until fully dried.) Expect this to come out a little tougher and drier than traditional beef jerky.

# Not Pemmican

*Traditional Pemmican is a high calorie meat-based traditional Native American food used to help sustain life during the long winters. I tried making pemmican one time, but I couldn't find any fresh deer meat, rendered beef fat, or dried currants at our local grocery store. Plus, I'm all thumbs when it comes to using a mortar and pestle. This recipe will have to do for now.*

*Makes 4 servings*
*2,195 calories*
*112 calories/ounce*

**Ingredients**
1 pound ground beef
4 cups spinach
1 medium onion, diced
½ cup sunflower seed kernels, raw, unsalted
1 cup raisins
½ cup ground flaxseed
¼ cup tomato paste
1 tablespoon salt
2 teaspoons liquid smoke

Place all ingredients in a blender or food processor. Pulse until ingredients are a smooth paste. You may need to scrape down sides of blender or food processor to ensure all ingredients are incorporated.

Add mixture into a jerky gun and put strips of jerky mixture directly onto dehydrator tray. If you don't have a jerky gun, spread mixture ¼ inch thick on parchment paper that has been cut to fit your dehydrator tray.

Dehydrate for about 5 hours or until the jerky is dried out. (You can speed up the dehydration time by cutting the partially dried jerky into smaller strips, then continuing to dehydrate until fully dried.) Expect this to come out a little tougher and drier than traditional beef jerky.

# Vegan + Gluten-free Pepperoni

*Even if you're not vegan or gluten-free, this recipe is worth making. It's healthier than the standard pack of pepperoni, and it's a fun companion to Flax Crackers (p. 57) and Hand-Rubbed Artisan Cheese (p. 66).*

Makes 2 rolls of pepperoni
532 calories
97 calories/ounce

### Ingredients

1 cup oats
¼ cup ground flaxseed
¼ cup nutritional yeast
¼ cup tomato paste
¼ cup water
2 teaspoons salt
2 teaspoons liquid smoke
1 teaspoon ground black pepper
1 teaspoon garlic powder

For added heat, add 1 teaspoon of red pepper flakes.

Mix all ingredients in a medium bowl and stir until combined. Divide dough in half and place each half on a piece of parchment paper or aluminum foil. Using the parchment paper or wet fingers, shape the dough into a log approximately 6–8 inches long.

Once the dough is shaped, wrap the parchment paper around the dough, then twist the ends of the parchment paper tightly and fold them under.

At this point there are two different ways you can "cure" this pepperoni:

**Stovetop:** In a double boiler, steam the wrapped pepperoni for 45 minutes.

**Pressure cooker:** Place 1 cup of water in the pressure cooker. Place the steamer tray inside and set the wrapped pepperoni on the tray. Cook on high pressure for 15 minutes. Quick-release or natural-release the pressure.

Remove pepperoni and unwrap slightly to allow steam to escape. Cool before slicing.

# Breads + Crackers + Chips

Breads, crackers, and chips are like little edible flatbed trucks that load up on things like cheese, jam, and peanut butter, then deliver them straight to your face at 60 miles per hour.

In this section, you'll find flavorful crackers and chips that come together in a matter of minutes, balanced out by two bread recipes that take part of your Saturday afternoon. Please—don't be afraid of the two bread recipes (Vollkornbrot Whole Rye Bread, p. 59; and Fruit and Nut Crostini, p. 60). I wouldn't have included them if they weren't worth your time.

And, I'll let you in on a little behind-the-scenes secret. When we were prepping the manuscript for *Trail Grazing*, we accidentally had one extra recipe. We looked for which one to cut, and there wasn't one from this chapter that I was willing to part with. (The recipe that didn't make the cut was the Chile Lime Pepitas from the Nuts + Seeds section. The test batch is still sitting on our pantry shelf… alone.)

# Plantain Chips

*It looks like a banana but tastes like a potato. And when you slice a plantain thinly and work some microwave magic, snacky things start to happen.*

*Makes 1 cup of chips*
*258 calories*
*95 calories/ounce*

**Ingredients**
1 green plantain
1 teaspoon oil
salt to taste

The recipe calls for a teaspoon of oil—and any kind will do, including Szechuan hot chili oil.

Peeling the plantain is the trickiest part. I like to use a vegetable peeler and peel one strip of plantain peel until I can see the plantain fruit. Once you get inside, it's much easier to get the rest of the peel off.

Using a mandolin or a knife, cut the peeled plantain into thin slices. Thinner is better.

Do not add the oil and salt yet! You'll do that *after* the plantains have dried out. You're not trying to "fry" the plantain chips in the microwave, you're simply drying them out.

In three batches, lay slices on parchment-lined microwave-safe plate. Do not overlap slices. Microwave for one minute on high. Move the chips into a pile in the center of the plate. Continue to microwave in 15- to 30-second intervals, "fluffing" the pile of chips each time until the they start to dry, but not too brown.

Toss with oil and salt.

Store chips an airtight container.

# Flax Crackers

*These simple crackers are great for eating with a packet of almond butter or some cheese (see Hand-Rubbed Artisan Cheese, p. 66). This recipe makes one serving of crackers—which contains about 12 grams of fiber!*

*Makes one serving of crackers*
*120 calories*
*120 calories/ounce*

**Ingredients**
¼ cup ground flaxseed
2 tablespoons water
⅛ teaspoon salt

Mix ground flaxseed, water, and salt. Let sit for 5 minutes until the seeds have absorbed all the water and a thick dough forms. If you skip this step, the dough will stick to the parchment.

Place the mixture on an 8×8-inch piece of parchment paper. Place another piece of parchment paper on top and roll dough into a 7-inch circle. Remove top piece of parchment. Using a pizza cutter or knife, score dough into 1-inch squares.

Place parchment with uncooked crackers on a plate and microwave for 2 minutes. Remove from microwave and break up crackers. Return to microwave to cook for another 30 seconds. Remove plate from microwave and leave crackers on plate to crisp as they cool.

Store crackers in an airtight container.

# Veggie Crackers

*How do we have the audacity to call these "Veggie Crackers," when there's not a veggie to be seen in the ingredient list? The secret, my friend, is in the seasoning blend. Most salt-free seasoning blends have a solid line-up of vegetables, herbs, spices, and even fruit peels. The seasoning blends that most grocery stores carry include carrots, onions, tomatoes, and celery. That's veggie enough for me!*

*Makes one serving of crackers*
*140 calories*
*127 calories/ounce*

**Ingredients**

2 tablespoons chia seeds
2 tablespoons ground flaxseed
2 tablespoons water
1 tablespoon nutritional yeast
½ teaspoon salt-free seasoning blend (like Mrs. Dash)
less than ¼ teaspoon salt

Nutritional yeast is an important ingredient in this recipe. It's what gives the crackers a cheesy, savory flavor.

Mix all ingredients in a small bowl. Let sit for 5 minutes until the seeds have absorbed all the water and a thick dough forms. If you skip this step, the dough will stick to the parchment.

Place the mixture on an 8×8-inch piece of parchment paper. Place another piece of parchment paper on top and roll dough into a 7-inch circle. Remove top piece of parchment. Using a pizza cutter or knife, score dough into 1-inch squares.

Place parchment with uncooked crackers on a plate and microwave for 2 minutes. Remove from microwave and break up crackers. Return to microwave to cook for another 30 seconds. Remove plate from microwave and leave crackers on plate to crisp as they cool.

Store crackers in an airtight container.

# Vollkornbrot Whole Rye Bread

*Our family hosted a German exchange student and learned quickly that commercial American bread is nothing like what they have in Germany. Our US grocery store shelves are lined with bags of fluffy, puffy bread. Our German student explained that vollkornbrot is a more dense, flavorful bread that won't collapse if you accidentally sit on it—making it the perfect bread for your next backpacking trip.*

Makes one loaf
2,667 calories
102 calories/ounce

**Ingredients**

4 cups dark rye flour
2 cups warm water
2 teaspoons yeast
2 teaspoons salt
1 cup sunflower seed kernels, raw, unsalted
¼ cup millet (optional)

Mix yeast and water together until slightly foamy. In a stand mixer, add flour, yeast mixture, salt, and sunflower seeds. Mix until combined. Spread into a greased medium loaf pan and let sit, covered, for 1 hour until slightly risen. This loaf is very dense and moist and will not double in size.

Preheat oven and bake for 60 minutes at 350°F. Internal temperature of the bread should reach 200°F.

Cool completely (which may take several hours) and slice thinly, about ¼" per slice. Wrap and store in freezer or refrigerator until ready to eat.

If you want to experiment with a small batch of this bread, make a half recipe and divide the dough into 2 mini loaf pans or make two small free-form loaves on a parchment-lined cookie sheet. Bake for 30 minutes. Internal temperature of the bread should reach 200°F.

# Fruit and Nut Crostini

*Fruit and Nut Crostini has an identical twin cousin named "fruitcake." They may "laugh alike and walk alike," but the differences are important. Crostini isn't boozy, and it most definitely has enough self-worth to avoid being re-gifted. It's thinly sliced and oven dried, which makes it delightfully crispy yet firm enough to hold up to a smear of schmear.*

Makes 32 crackers
2,231 calories
107 calories/ounce

**Ingredients**

½ cup whole wheat flour
2 tablespoons sugar
¼ teaspoon baking soda
¼ teaspoon baking powder
¼ teaspoon salt
1 cup dates, finely chopped
½ cup dried apricots, finely chopped
1¾ cups walnut pieces
2 eggs

This recipe takes some extra time, but it's a fun one. Save half for yourself, and share the other half with a hiker friend.

Preheat oven to 300 degrees F.

In a large bowl, combine flour, sugar, baking soda, baking powder, and salt. Add chopped dried fruit and nuts, and stir to combine. Add eggs and mix well.

Line an 8×4-inch medium loaf pan with parchment paper. Pour in the batter and smooth the top with the back of a spoon to flatten the loaf. Bake for 1 hour, until browned on the edges. Remove from pan and let the loaf cool (about 1 hour).

Using a sharp serrated knife, cut loaf into thin slices (¼ inch or less). Spread slices out on a parchment-lined baking sheet. Bake at 250°F for 30 minutes on each side. They will still be somewhat "bendy" after they come out of the oven, but they will crisp up as they cool.

Store in an airtight container. Serve with a 1-ounce cream cheese packet.

# Microwave Muffins

Remember back when cupcakes were a big, big thing? Cupcakes were très trendy! There were cupcake shops all over the place. Cupcakes even got their own TV show—*Cupcake Wars*! Yet through it all, the real star was *always* the sturdy, stable, wholesome muffin. No fancy frosting, no dazzling sprinkles, and no finicky uptown cult following.

Muffins have loved you the whole time.

These muffins want to come backpacking with you. But they know you're busy. Too busy to preheat an oven—and they understand that. So these muffins aren't made in the oven. They're made in the microwave.

Quick tip: if you want these muffins to come together faster than a goodbye party for a North Korean dictator, then pre-mix all the dry ingredients together, store in a zip top bag, and label the bag with what wet ingredients need to be added (and any other cooking instructions.)

# Trail Cred Muffins

*These muffins couldn't be easier—and they're loads healthier than anything from your grocery store snack aisle. If you're suspicious of baked goods that come from a microwave, try these out and be pleasantly and permanently surprised. Bringing these on your next hike will give you plenty of trail cred.*

Makes 6 muffins

1,030 calories

105 calories/ounce

**Ingredients**

1 cup whole wheat flour

¼ cup brown sugar

¼ cup walnut pieces

2 tablespoons unsweetened shredded coconut

1 tablespoon ground flaxseed

½ tablespoon baking powder

½ teaspoon cinnamon

¼ teaspoon salt

½ cup water

2 tablespoons oil

Line 6 silicone baking cups with paper muffin liners. If you don't have silicone baking cups, you can line 6 wide-mouth half-pint mason jars with paper muffin liners.

Mix all ingredients. Divide evenly among muffin liners.

Place muffins in microwave and cook for 2 minutes. Check the muffins. If the tops spring back and there are no moist spots, the muffins are done. Remove the ones that are done, and continue to cook the remainder in 30-second intervals.

When the muffins are done cooking, there will be hot condensed water between the liner and the container. Be careful that you don't get burned!

When cooled, place muffins in an empty Pringles can to protect your precious baked goods.

The best way to store muffins while on the trail is in a Pringles potato crisps can. It's hard-sided, so the muffins are protected. The standard size Pringles can holds about six muffins.

# Blueberry Muffins

*Mmmm… the classic blueberry muffin. Full of whole grains and berries.*

*Makes 6 muffins*
*966 calories*
*101 calories/ounce*

**Ingredients**

1 cup whole wheat flour
¼ cup brown sugar
1 tablespoon ground flaxseed
½ tablespoon baking powder
¼ teaspoon salt
½ cup water
2 tablespoons oil
1 teaspoon vanilla
½ cup blueberries, fresh or thawed

Line 6 silicone baking cups with paper muffin liners. If you don't have silicone baking cups, you can line 6 wide-mouth half-pint mason jars with paper muffin liners.

Mix dry ingredients together. Add water, oil, and vanilla to dry ingredients and mix well. Add blueberries and stir gently.

Divide evenly among muffin liners.

Place muffins in microwave and cook for 2 minutes. Check the muffins. If the tops spring back and there are no moist spots, the muffins are done. Remove the ones that are done, and continue to cook the remainder in 30 second intervals.

When the muffins are done cooking, there will be hot condensed water between the liner and the container. Be careful that you don't get burned!

# Cheesy Italian Muffins

*These muffins have all the flavor of a cheesy slice of pizza, but without all the drippy sauce. Feel free to pack that separately to use as a dip for these muffins.*

*Makes 6 muffins*
*705 calories*
*99 calories/ounce*

### Ingredients
½ cup whole wheat flour
¼ cup grated Parmesan cheese
1 tablespoon brown sugar
1 tablespoon baking powder
½ tablespoon ground flaxseed
¼ teaspoon salt
¼ teaspoon Italian seasoning
¼ cup water
1 tablespoon oil
20 slices pepperoni, diced

Line 6 silicone baking cups with paper muffin liners. If you don't have silicone baking cups, you can line 6 wide-mouth half-pint mason jars with paper muffin liners.

Mix all ingredients. Divide evenly among muffin liners.

Place muffins in microwave and cook for 2 minutes. Check the muffins. If the tops spring back and there are no moist spots, the muffins are done. Remove the ones that are done, and continue to cook the remainder in 30 second intervals.

When the muffins are done cooking, there will be hot condensed water between the liner and the container. Be careful that you don't get burned!

When cooled, place muffins in an empty Pringles can to protect your precious baked goods.

# Cheese

Most of the time our precious cheese is stored at home in a refrigerator—but backpackers know that cheese can have a wild and exciting life outside of the cold, confining walls of the Frigidaire. Cheese is a backpacker's secret weapon when it comes to savory snacks and on-the-go meals on the trail. Cheese can make the most out of a cracker (see Flax Crackers, p. 57), but most cheese lovers are OK with no cracker at all.

Backpackers have a special relationship with cheese. We know that it sweats and breathes, just like we do. And it can get a little funky smelling, just like us. We're aware of its limits, and we're not afraid to cut off the mold to get to the gold. Cheese longs for adventure, just like us.

But what if you're a little reluctant to take a "perishable" on the trail? Here's the perfect opportunity to exercise your "risk muscle." To have success with cheese on the trail, take hard or semi-hard cheese with a low moisture content, and wrap it in a layer of parchment, then store in a plastic bag. And if you *must* pack along something softer, like Brie or goat cheese, it's best to consume it within the first day.

# Hand-Rubbed Artisan Cheese

*Yes, you can take a block of plain ol' cheese on your next hike. But imagine the looks on the faces of all the chipmunks (and hikers) in the forest when they see you unwrap your flavor-infused Hand-Rubbed Artisan Cheese. They will go cah-ray-zee.*

*Makes 4 2-ounce blocks of hand-rubbed cheese*
*880 calories*
*110 calories/ounce*

**Ingredients**

8 ounces Monterey Jack (or other mild, semi-hard cheese)
4 tablespoons seasoning blend

Cut cheese into 4 equal blocks. Measure seasoning blend onto a plate or cutting board. Press each side of the cheese into the seasoning blend, being sure to evenly coat each side.

Wrap cheese tightly in parchment paper, label, and store in a plastic bag in refrigerator until ready to bring on the trail.

Your local grocery store will have a good selection of seasoning blends. I tried both salted and salt-free varieties and was pleased with both. My favorites were a chili lime seasoning salt, a no-salt zesty seasoning blend, and a lemon pepper seasoning salt.

# "Everything Bagel" Mozzarella Cheese Sticks

*"Everything bagels" are plain bagels topped with a seasoning mix that includes onion, garlic, sesame seeds, and poppy seeds. This simple recipe uses the brilliant flavor combo from "everything bagels" and hitches some mozzarella cheese sticks to that wagon. Now you have everything you ever wanted.*

*Makes 2 cheese sticks*
*160 calories*
*80 calories/ounce*

### Ingredients
2 mozzarella cheese sticks
1 teaspoon dried chopped onion
½ teaspoon sesame seeds
½ teaspoon poppy seeds
¼ teaspoon garlic powder

Measure last 4 ingredients onto a cutting board and mix with fingers.

Unwrap mozzarella cheese sticks and roll each one in the seed mixture, pressing firmly so that the seasonings adhere to the cheese.

Wrap both cheese sticks together in a piece of parchment paper and store in a plastic bag. Store in a refrigerator until ready to bring on the trail.

# About the Author

Podcasts are usually done by people who are experts in their field. They know a lot, and they have a lot to say. I host a backpacking podcast called *The First 40 Miles*. However, I'm not an expert. I'm a beginner backpacker. I haven't solo hiked the Pacific Crest Trail or sawed off a frost-bitten limb with a credit card. I have never eaten raw squirrel meat or slept under a blanket of pine needles and steaming bear dung. I haven't been stranded for weeks in the woods with only a knife—and a camera crew.

But, I have discovered a simple love of hiking and backpacking. And it all happened in the first 40 miles. In 2014, my husband was preparing for his first weeklong backpacking trip in a long while. I became interested in everything he was learning. Then, a week before the trip, Josh's trip leader pulled me aside at a wedding reception and asked, "Would you like to go?" Something sparked inside of me! I went from zero to ready in seven days. My first 40 miles was spent circumnavigating Mount Hood on the Timberline Trail.

I want to approach backpacking with creativity, because there are few things that require as much creative thinking, imagination, inventiveness, improvisation, insight, and intuition as the act of strapping 30 pounds to your back and disappearing into the thick woods.

—Heather Legler

# Index

baking dish, 10

Beef + Bean Burrito Jerky, 49

Beef + Veggie Jerky, 46

Berry + Beet Fruit Leather, 32

Big Batch Lunch Lady Bars, 23

Black Bean "Nuts", 42

Black Bean Brownies, 24

blender, 10

Blueberry Muffins, 61

bread, 53

Brownie Bark, 25

California Jerky, 48

calories, 8

cheese, 63

Cheesy Italian Muffins, 62

chips, 53

Cocoa Dusted Almonds, 43

Coconut + Curry Cashews, 39

crackers, 53

Cucumber + Lime Fruit Leather, 34

dehydrator, 11

equipment, 10

"Everything Bagel" Mozzarella Cheese Sticks, 65

Flax Crackers, 55

food processor, 10

Fruit + Nut Bars, 18

Fruit and Nut Crostini, 58

fruit leather, 29

Go-To Granola Bars, 16

granola bars, 15

half-sheet pan, 11

Hand-Rubbed Artisan Cheese, 64

Hikers' Taffy, 27

jerky, 45

knife, 11

loaf pan, 10

microwave, 11

microwave-safe bowl, 10

Mini Chia Bars, 21

Montezuma's Chocolate Drops, 44

muffins, 59

Naturally Sweet + Chewy Baked Bars, 20

Not Pemmican, 51

nuts, 37

parchment paper, 11

Perfect Crunchy Granola Bars, 17

Plantain Chips, 54

Quick Chocolate Caramel Bars, 19

Roasted Squash Seeds, 38

seeds, 37

Sesame Ginger Pecans, 41

Simple Fruit Leather, 30

Smoky Maple BBQ Nuts, 40

spatula, 11

storage, 12

Thanksgiving Turkey Jerky, 50

"Thoughtful" Bars, 22

Trail Cred Muffins, 60

Vanilla Orange Fruit Leather, 33

Vegan + Gluten-free Pepperoni, 52

Veggie Crackers, 56

Vollkornbrot Whole Rye Bread, 57

Whole Food Truffles, 26

Yogurt Fruit Leather, 35

Printed in Great Britain
by Amazon